The Challenge of
SUPPLYING
ENERGY

Gail B. Haines

✦Environmental Issues Series✦

E N S L O W   P U B L I S H E R S,   I N C.

Bloy St. & Ramsey Avenue
Box 777
Hillside, N.J. 07205
U.S.A.

P.O. Box 38
Aldershot
Hants GU12 6BP
U.K.

Library of Congress Cataloging-in-Publication Data

Haines, Gail B.
    The challenge of supplying energy / Gail B. Haines.
        p. cm.—(Environmental issues series)
    Summary: Presents the current state of our energy supply,
discussing how energy works, how it is developed, and who uses it.
    ISBN 0-89490-269-5
    1. Power resources—Juvenile literature. [1. Power resources.
2. Energy development.] I. Title. II. Series: Environmental
issues series (Hillside, N.J.)
TJ163.23.H35 1991
333.79—dc20   89-28498
                                                                    CIP
                                                                     AC

Printed in the United States of America

10 9 8 7 6 5 4 3 2 1

Photo Credits:
Courtesy of Bonneville Power Administration, 6, 10,14, 17, 24, 33, 37, 39,
46, 48, 51; Department of Energy, 12, 53; Point Defiance Zoo & Aquarium,
photo by Mel Wood, 28; Washington State Capital Museum, 4.

Cover Photograph:
Courtesy of Bonneville Power Administration.

Contents

1

Energy Supply

Think about a hot July day without air conditioning. Imagine shivering under six blankets on a February night with the heat shut down. Pretend you must walk five miles to school because the buses and cars have run out of gasoline—and so have all the gas stations. These situations have actually occurred in the past, and they can happen again. Energy is very important—but it is not guaranteed.

Where Does Energy Come From?

Prehistoric people depended on the energy from their bodies. They hunted, built their own homes and tools, and sometimes traveled hundreds of miles using only the power in their arms and legs. Today, that kind of energy isn't enough.

Over the centuries, people discovered new sources of energy. Animals could pull and carry, but they had to be trained, fed, and cared for. Fire could cook food, warm homes, and run steam engines. It could even be used to make electricity. But fire needed fuel—lots of fuel: from piles of dry sticks, to mountains of heavy logs, to tons and tons of coal dug out of the ground. Fire from wood or coal also polluted the air with smoke and soot and generated giant piles of ashes.

5

Next, people discovered that falling water could turn paddlewheels and run engines. It could also be used to generate electricity. Water-power didn't require fuel, but building giant dams to trap water cost a lot of money. Also, dams may spoil the view and make life difficult for fish.

About one hundred and thirty years ago, people discovered a spectacular new energy source. Oil and gas piped out of the ground opened up a world of new energy uses, such as home lighting and fueling automobiles. They also brought new problems: high cost, pollution, and the worry that the supply could eventually run out.

One more discovery, less than fifty years old, provided what people hoped would be an economical source of enough energy to last forever. They learned how to build huge nuclear power plants, which could harness the energy locked inside radioactive atoms. Unfortunately, the new

Falling water as a form of energy.

source of power cost far more than its investors expected and left behind dangerous and long-lasting garbage. No energy source was—or is—perfect.

The Big Five

The big five sources of energy—coal, oil, gas, falling water, and nuclear power, are the main power producers in today's world. Along with smaller contributions from the sun, the wind, the heat inside the earth, and several other sources, they are the energy supply which keeps civilization moving.

What Is an Energy Crisis?

When something goes wrong with one of our main power sources, an energy crisis is the result. Not enough energy is available in the places where people need it. Energy crises have happened before when wars cut the supply of oil, when droughts shut off water power, and when coal or nuclear plants failed or were not allowed to operate. People anticipate more crises in the future, because energy is not free and many sources are limited. Each energy source has advantages and disadvantages, pluses and minuses. Providing a safe and constant energy supply is a complex problem. The people who use energy can be part of the solution, but first they need to understand the issues. They need a knowledge of science, which explains what energy is and where it comes from. They need an understanding of technology, which produces and distributes energy. Finally, they need an aware-ness of the ways energy affects society and people. Science, technology, and society must combine to find answers.

2

Energy Science:
How Energy Works

Picture a huge river, cascading over a waterfall. Picture glowing coal in a factory's furnace. Picture a dog chasing his tail, and sunshine beaming down. All these scenes show sources of energy.

Now, imagine a giant tractor-trailer speeding down the freeway. Think about a man switching on a lamp, a dog bringing in the newspaper, or sunshine melting ice on a frozen lake. These scenes show energy at work.

The word *energy* means different things to different people, but to scientists, energy is the ability to do work. Work can be anything from picking up a pencil, to providing electricity for a whole city, to firing satellites into orbit around the earth. Every kind of work takes energy, and all that energy has to come from somewhere.

Where Does Energy Come From?

Simply stated, energy comes from matter in motion, or moving things. Matter in motion always produces energy, whether the moving matter involved is waterfalls, burning lumps of coal, pellets of radioactive uranium, or the atoms and molecules in your own bones and muscles.

Different substances produce energy in different ways, but they all use motion to do work.

Scientists list six basic kinds of energy. Your arms give *mechanical* energy to a basketball. A truck on the freeway gets *chemical* energy from the gasoline pumped into its tank. A hot burner on the stove supplies *thermal* energy to a skillet of hamburgers, while it draws *electrical* energy from a socket in the wall. The sun uses *radiant* energy to melt snow, generate a breeze, or cause roses to grow, but it gets its own *nuclear* energy from reactions happening inside the nuclei of its own atoms.

Law of Conservation of Energy

Sometimes these six kinds of energy overlap in the same energy source, and they often change back and forth from one to another. In fact, to scientists, all energy ever does is change from one form to another. It never simply appears or disappears. Scientists call this fact the Law of Conservation of Energy, which states that energy is never created or destroyed—it simply moves from one kind or one place to another. The law includes matter, which is a form of energy.

People usually find that idea confusing, because energy and matter, too, seem to come and go all the time. You may feel, when you get tired, that your energy is all used up. You can see a campfire die because its logs have turned to ashes. But what you see and feel is not the complete energy story. All of your personal energy and all of the fire's matter and energy still exist—if you know where and how to look for them.

Physicists and chemists are experts at looking for matter and energy. They can actually collect all the smoke and steam that come from a fire, plus all the ashes left over, weigh them and demonstrate that the whole collection weighs exactly as much as the logs did to start with. They can also measure every tiny bit of energy the fire produces to warm hands and air, to cook dinner, and even to light up the campsite. That measurement will show exactly the same amount

9

of energy as the energy stored inside the fuel to start with. Hard to believe—but true.

The Laws of Thermodynamics

The Law of Conservation of Energy, which scientists also call the First Law of Thermodynamics, seems to defy common sense. If energy is never used up or destroyed, why do we keep needing more of it? Why can't the same energy be used again and again?

The Second Law of Thermodynamics answers this question. As energy changes form, some of it becomes unavailable for use. Energy is lost to further use because it becomes useless heat. Every time any kind of energy is used to do work, some of it spreads out into the atmosphere. It still exists, but it has become unavailable to do any further work, ever. Scientists have a special name for this inevitable energy escape. They call it entropy.

Entropy is a complicated mathematical concept, but the main idea is easy to understand. Every time energy changes form, a fraction of it is lost to entropy. Trying to recapture the missing energy always

Freeway traffic gets chemical energy from gasoline.

takes more energy than it recovers. Nothing can stop entropy loss, not even the most careful energy conservation. Entropy is like a tax that must be paid on every exchange of energy.

Because entropy exists, "new" energy is constantly needed to keep civilization moving. But since the Law of Conservation of Energy says no new energy can ever be created, where does it come from? The answer lies in the action of the six kinds of energy. As each changes from one kind to another, stored energy is released to do work.

Mechanical Energy

Mechanical energy comes from moving objects, so this form is easy to observe. Watch a giant crane lift an automobile into the air or crank a pulley to drag a boat out of the water. Pitch a ball and strike the batter out—or see the batter hit your pitch out of the park. Feel the earth move while a bulldozer turns a hillside into a ditch. Mechanical means using tools or machinery to get work done.

Millions of different things can serve as tools. A pulley, a bat, and a bulldozer blade are obvious tools. A pencil is a writing tool, and so is a typewriter and a word processor.

Scientists divide mechanical and other kinds of energy into two forms, kinetic and potential. Kinetic energy is motion at work. Potential energy is motion in storage. The amount of mechanical energy an object has is the total of these two forms.

The simplest example of a kinetic/potential energy transfer is a tennis ball tossed straight up into the air. At first, the moving ball has all kinetic energy, the energy of motion. As it rises, it slows down. Kinetic energy is being turned into potential.

Finally, the ball stops dead and hangs, for a fraction of a second, in the air. It has lost all kinetic energy, because it is no longer moving, but its mid-air position gives it as much potential energy as the amount of kinetic energy it started with. As the ball falls, it loses potential energy and gains its kinetic energy back. Students in physics classes can calculate exactly how much of each form of energy the ball has at every point in its path. In theory, a perfectly elastic ball could bounce up and down forever, trading potential and kinetic energy back and forth. In reality, that can't happen. Eventually it stops. Entropy wins. A bow drawn back to shoot has potential energy, which turns to kinetic as the arrow flies. A waterfall has massive potential energy at the top, with tons of water in position to fall. As the water drops, it loses potential energy and gains kinetic, which it spends as it crashes onto the rocks below.

Mechanical energy involves more than just trading potential and kinetic energy back and forth. Machines can't create energy, but they can make using it more efficient. Consider this: which takes less energy—carrying a sack of sand or pushing it in a wheelbarrow? Tools make work easier by demanding less energy to get a job done.

Almost any time objects move, mechanical energy is involved. A

Trapped water has potential energy. As water falls, the energy changes to kinetic.

quarterback uses his arm as a football-throwing tool and a champion skater spins her body like a top. The wind pushes with mechanical energy when it moves a sailboat or stirs up a tornado. Places of work from farms to factories all depend upon mechanical energy.

Chemical Energy

Chemical energy comes from within molecules. Almost everything on earth is made of molecules, which are groups of atoms—from two to many thousand—bonded together. The chemical bonds which tie atoms together contain potential energy. When those bonds are broken, they release energy to do work.

A wood fire is a simple demonstration of chemical energy at work. A burning log gives off energy, which you can see as light and feel as heat. That energy, which originally came from the sun, may have been stored for years inside the trunk of a tree. These are the steps in that process:

1. The tree grows from a seed, combining oxygen from the air and nutrients from the soil with water to form molecules of wood and bark and leaf. These combinations are chemical reactions which take in energy. They get that energy from sunlight.

2. The tree is cut down into firewood. But before it can start to burn, it has to take in more energy, in the form of heat. A match lights some paper or twigs and they ignite some larger kindling. Finally, the log catches.

3. Next, chemical reactions begin to happen inside the log. Burning, which chemists call combustion, breaks down the chemical bonds inside the molecules of wood, mixes them with air, and recombines the same atoms into new molecules. The chemical bonds in the new molecules have less potential energy than the old ones. The extra energy becomes heat and light.

Most chemical reactions are harder to see, but they all produce energy in the same way. Energy is taken in when chemical bonds form.

13

The energy is stored, then given off later when the bonds break. That is why all the matter in a campfire, if it could be recollected, would still weigh the same. None of the atoms are gone, they have simply been recombined.

Chemical energy powers a barbecue fire, a moving bulldozer, and all the cars on the road. From the sun's energy stored in food, it also provides the power to a quarterback's arm, a racehorse's legs, and your working brain.

Thermal Energy

Thermal energy is the energy of moving molecules. All molecules are moving all the time, even in the most stable-looking solid, but the more energy they contain, the faster they move. And as they move, they bump into each other, passing along kinetic energy. The trade always goes from faster molecules to slower ones—never the other way.

A thermometer measures the thermal energy in water.

14

Molecules are too small to see in action, but you can demonstrate the effects of what they do with a mercury thermometer and a pan of lukewarm water. Dip the mercury end of the thermometer into the water and watch the measuring line. Molecules in the water touch the glass and deliver energy. Molecules in the glass bump molecules in the mercury and transfer more energy. Molecules in the mercury move faster and spread apart, taking up more space. The thread of mercury rises. Moving molecules give off energy as heat, and the faster molecules move, the more heat they give off. You can feel heat if you put your hand near a hot radiator. Air molecules touch the radiator, gain heat, and transfer that energy to make the molecules in your skin move faster.

Everything has thermal energy, even icicles. Even at hundreds of degrees below freezing, scientific laboratories can never quite remove the last tiny bit of kinetic energy (actually, the last bit of entropy) from a molecule. But because the transfer of energy from molecule to molecule only goes one way, from higher temperature to lower, thermal energy is useful only when one subject is hotter than another. In other words, a hot hamburger can melt cheese; a cold bun cannot.

Heat can do far more than cook food. Thermal energy can power engines and rockets, generate electricity, and run machines, as well as warm homes and offices. All of the other five kinds of energy can easily be converted to thermal energy.

Because energetic molecules keep bumping into cooler ones, thermal energy is especially vulnerable to entropy loss. While a hot burner is supplying thermal energy to fry a hamburger, it is also heating the skillet, the air in the room, and anything else its molecules touch. Thermal energy transfers usually waste more energy than they use.

Electrical Energy

Electrical energy comes from tiny charged particles called electrons. Electrons are the outside part of every atom, whirling around the nucleus somewhat like planets around the sun. Protons are particles which make up part of the nucleus of an atom, and every normal atom has an equal number of protons and electrons.

Every electron carries a tiny negative electrical charge. Every proton carries an equal-size positive electrical charge. That's why atoms are usually electrically neutral. The charges balance.

When energy knocks electrons loose, they can move to another atom. They can even travel from atom to atom, carrying energy as they go. Electrical current refers to a large number of electrons, passing kinetic energy through a metal wire.

Electrons are easy to knock loose. Run a plastic comb several times through one side of your hair, and the comb will pick up millions of extra electrons. It becomes charged with negative electricity. Hold the comb close to the other side of your hair. Usually, nothing happens, because the hair is electrically neutral. Now hold the comb close to the combed side. Because you removed some electrons, the hair has become charged with positive electricity. Strands of hair fly up to touch the comb. The hair's positively charged atoms, out of balance, are attracted to their lost electrons.

Electricity is a convenient way to move energy from one place to another. Heat and falling water can't run a washing machine one hundred miles away. Neither can sunlight or gasoline, but they can each run a mechanical device designed to set electrons free and send them flowing, or simply vibrating, along a wire as electricity. At the other end of the wire, an electric motor turns that electrical energy back into the mechanical energy needed to wash clothes.

In Europe and many parts of the world, electricity moves by direct current (DC). Electrons actually flow from atom to atom through wires, carrying kinetic energy. The United States, Canada, and some other countries use alternating current (AC), where the electrons move back and forth, first one way and then the other, switching direction fifty or sixty times a second. Only their kinetic energy flows through the wire.

Electricity powers millions of things people use every day, from hair dryers to computers to elevated trains. It provides light and heat and the energy for tools, appliances, and machines.

Radiant Energy

Light is pure energy—easy to see, but difficult for scientists to explain. The most obvious source of light is the sun, which sends huge amounts of radiant energy to earth every day. Sunlight radiates through ninety-three million miles of empty space with enough strength to warm the earth, light up the sky, and sometimes even burn skin. Most of the energy used on earth originally radiated from the sun.

Light has confused scientists for centuries because it acts sometimes like a wave and sometimes like a stream of super-tiny particles. Today's physicists think light is both at once—a beam of massless packets of energy which can make waves through air or space the way a boat makes waves move through water. They call particles of light *photons*.

Vibrating electrons pass kinetic energy through wires.

17

Visible light—the kind that can be seen by people or animals—comes in all the colors of the rainbow, or with all those colors mixed together into ordinary colorless light. The colors are easy to see when sunlight passes through a prism or through raindrops to create a rainbow. Different colors travel in different wavelengths, each with different amounts of energy.

Red light, at the top of the rainbow, moves in the longest waves and carries the least energy. Invisible waves even longer than red light give the heat to sunlight, cook food in microwave ovens, and carry radio sounds. Violet light has the shortest visible wavelength, and the most energy. Shorter, invisible waves produce X-rays.

Light is the fastest-moving kind of energy. In fact, the speed of light, 186,282.4 miles per second, is a quantity scientists use to represent the ultimate speed limit. No kind of matter can travel that fast.

Radiant energy is used to light houses, buildings, and streets. It sends radio and television signals all over the world, bouncing off satellites and traveling for thousands of miles. It tracks airplanes and takes pictures of bones. It helps plants grow. Radiant energy from the sun makes life on earth possible.

Nuclear Energy

Because nuclear energy comes from inside atoms, it was first called atomic energy. The name was changed, because scientists realized the energy comes from changes inside the nucleus, or center of an atom—not just in the atom itself.

Nuclear energy happens two ways. *Fission* means breaking apart, and nuclear fission happens when large nuclei split in two, giving off a spray of tiny particles and huge amounts of energy. *Fusion* means sticking together, and nuclear fusion forces two nuclei to combine, giving off vast amounts of energy.

The first five kinds of energy: mechanical, chemical, thermal, electrical, and radiant, all do work by releasing energy which already exists. They don't create energy, they only move it around. Nuclear fission and fusion cannot create energy either, but they do change a tiny bit of matter into energy. This is the process:

1. A nucleus consists of protons and neutrons. Each nucleus may have from one to over a hundred protons, and each element, or kind of atom, has a different number. Hydrogen has one proton, for instance, and uranium has ninety-two. Every nucleus—except for hydrogen—has an equal or larger number of particles called neutrons. Neutrons are neutral; they have no electrical charge.

2. Since each proton carries positive electricity, protons tend to repel, or push each other away. If a nucleus were made only of protons, it would fly apart.

3. Neutrons help hold a nucleus together, but they can't do the job alone. So every atom transfers a tiny part of its mass into a kind of nuclear superglue. The more mass transferred, the more stable the atom. Elements such as iron (26 protons) and lead (82 protons) are very stable. They don't come apart.

4. Scientists can calculate a number called the packing fraction for each kind of atom, to measure how much mass is gluing each nucleus together. Middle-sized iron and lead have low packing fractions, which means lots of glue. Very large and very small atoms, such as hydrogen and uranium, have much larger fractions. The bonds gluing them together are weaker. They can be broken.

5. Large, unstable atoms can be split, becoming two smaller, more stable atoms. All the protons and neutrons are still there, but a tiny bit of the mass holding them together—their packing fraction—turns into energy. One of the world's best known physicists, Albert Einstein, was the first to calculate how much energy is given off when fission happens. His famous formula, $E=mc^2$, says that energy equals the amount of mass times the velocity of light, multiplied by itself. Since the

19

velocity of light (see radiant energy), squared, is so great, a tiny speck of mass can turn into huge amounts of energy.

6. Hydrogen, with one proton, has the highest packing fraction of all, but it is too small to split. A special hydrogen atom can be fused to another hydrogen to form an atom called helium (2 protons). Helium has a much lower packing fraction. Some of the extra mass turns into energy. $E=mc^2$ tells how much. Nuclear fusion gives the sun and the other stars their enormous amounts of energy. Nuclear fusion also powers hydrogen bombs. So far, scientists have had trouble turning nuclear fusion into useful work.

Nuclear fission can come from radioactive atoms, which split apart all by themselves to release energy, or it can happen when physicists fire tiny particles, like bullets, at unstable atoms. Nuclear fission powered the original atomic bombs, and it provides the energy in nuclear power plants which generate electricity. It has been used to run nuclear submarines and other large ships. So far, scientists have not found a way to use nuclear fission in small ways.

Where Does Energy Come From?

All the energy the universe will ever have already exists. It is either stored, working, or wasted—turned into useless entropy. But a fresh supply is constantly arriving on earth, beamed down by the sun to add to the amount already here.

The goal of energy science is to transform energy into forms people can use. To do that, they have turned ideas about energy into action.

3

Energy Technology:
How Energy Is Developed

Picture a million people living in the suburbs, needing to get to work in the city. Imagine a cold winter and ten million houses with no fireplaces. Think about a ballgame in Cincinnati, that you want to watch in Seattle. Technology means "applied science," or using science to solve problems.

The five big sources of energy—coal, oil, gas, water, and nuclear power, produce 99 percent of the energy people use. Each one has certain advantages and disadvantages. No single source is best for everything.

Fossil Fuels

Coal, oil, and natural gas all come from sunlight collected millions of years ago. As ancient plants and animals grew, they built up energy-storing molecules. When they died, some were buried and preserved. As the fossilized remains of those plants and animals burn today, they give the sun's radiant energy back as chemical energy. The three fossil fuels provide more than 90 percent of the world's energy supply.

Coal

No one knows who first discovered the "black rock that burns," but coal was heating homes in China two thousand years ago. Geologists found that coal comes from ancient swampy jungles. As trees and vines and giant ferns died, they were buried under water and layers of sand and rock. Bacteria, tons of pressure, and millions of years turned the woody, leafy "muck" into solid layers of coal.

The physical qualities of coal vary from brown and crumbly to shiny black and hard, depending mainly on age. The element carbon— the material in pencil lead and the major element in your body—is always the main ingredient, combined with a mixture of materials from hydrogen and sulfur to poisonous metals. Almost every chemical element has been found in coal.

Scientists rank coal into four grades, according to the amount of carbon it contains. Anthracite coal, with the highest carbon content, is hard and black. It gives the most heat and costs most. The other grades: bituminous, subbituminous, and lignite, have progressively less carbon. They are also progressively softer and smokier to burn.

More than half the coal used in the United States is turned into electricity. Scientists use a steam turbine and a dynamo to convert it in these steps:

1. Coal is burned in a furnace called a boiler, converting chemical energy into thermal energy and turning water into superheated steam.

2. Expanding steam pushes the blades of a rotating wheel, like a giant electric fan. The wheel turns, producing mechanical energy to rotate a shaft inside an electric generator called a dynamo.

3. In the dynamo, mechanical energy spins a magnet between two other magnets, freeing billions of electrons. The electrons carry electrical energy, either as alternating or direct current, into wires and then away.

Because of entropy and other losses, only about 35–40 percent of the chemical energy in the coal gets to customers as electricity, from the most modern power plants. Engineers expect to burn about seven-tenths of a pound of bituminous coal for every kilowatt-hour of electricity they produce—enough power to light one 100-watt lightbulb for ten hours.

Coal's energy is also used directly as heat and in the furnaces in steel mills and other factories. Before coal can provide energy, it must be mined, cleaned, and transported.

Coal Mining

Years ago, miners—both men and boys—spent much of their lives in dark, deep holes in the ground and often died of accidents or of black lung, an illness caused by breathing coal dust. Another kind of mining used a bulldozer to strip grass and dirt off veins of coal lying close to the surface of the ground. It left millions of acres bare and brown, covered with deep, ugly scars. Mud and acid, from chemicals in the coal, polluted nearby rivers.

Mining for coal buried deep in the ground is still dangerous, but machinery, better ventilation, and sturdier mine construction have solved many of the problems. Strip miners now use power shovels big enough to dig out 300 tons of dirt and coal in one scoop. Mining companies are required to fix some of the damage this does by refilling the holes, putting back the topsoil, and replanting the ground. More than 60 percent of United States coal is strip mined.

Next, technologists use physical, chemical, and biological methods to clean the coal. Water jets jiggle lumps of coal around in a sieve. Magnetic separators pull out iron. Concentrating tables trap different-sized lumps and water, and swirling cyclones separate particles by size and weight.

Chemical cleaning goes after polluting chemicals inside the coal itself, especially sulfur. Sulfur, the Bible's brimstone, is a yellowish rocky element. Most of sulfur's chemical compounds are poisonous and bad-smelling, like the odor of rotten eggs. When coal is burned, sulfur mixes with oxygen to form sulfur dioxide (SO_2) and sulfur trioxide (SO_3), which float up in the air as smog and fall back down to earth as acid rain.

Forcing hydrogen through coal can remove some sulfur, and treatment with oxygen can remove more. Scientists have developed bacteria which can "eat" sulfur right out of the coal. The methods currently in use remove less than half.

Burning coal produces a major set of pollution problems. Smoke, soot, and ashes can blacken cities and the sky overhead. Smog and sour acid rain cause illness and damage the environment. Today most plants eliminate smoke by careful burning, but ashes and bits of metals and minerals—even some radioactive pollutants—still escape into the air by the ton. Filters try to remove sulfur compounds, but almost half

A generating plant burns coal to produce electricity.

gets through. Engineers hope that building taller smokestacks, higher into the air, will dilute the pollution. Leftover ashes, about 100,000 tons per plant per year, need storing somewhere.

More than a billion tons of coal are dug every year around the world. China produces most—about 960 million tons. In the United States, the second biggest producer, a year's supply of coal fills six million railroad cars. Coal is the most abundant fossil fuel in the world. Of the United States' unused fossil fuel supply, about 90 percent is buried coal.

The world supply of coal should last for another thousand years. It is less expensive than most other fuels, it can be turned into gases and gasolines to serve all kinds of energy needs, and most of its pollution problems can eventually be solved. Unfortunately, solving the pollution problems costs money, making coal power more and more expensive.

One major source of pollution from coal cannot be solved with the best cleaning methods. Coal burning, like any kind of burning, gives off carbon dioxide (CO_2). Carbon dioxide is the same gas you breathe out and trees and other plants take in. It is a normal part of air, but the energy industry—mainly from burning coal—pours billions of extra tons of it into the atmosphere.

Some scientists think all that extra CO_2 has a greenhouse effect, bringing new and dangerous changes into the environment. Planting trees to absorb the extra carbon dioxide is one idea, but experts say enough new trees to cover half the United States would be needed.

Oil

Petroleum, or crude oil, is the leading source of energy in the United States. It provides more than 40 percent of our total supply.

Geologists think most petroleum formed millions of years ago, as the bodies of tiny, one-celled plants and animals in and around the oceans sank and became buried by tons of sand and mud. Those ancient cells turned into a thick, black, oily material. Today it lies trapped in the cracks and spaces between rocks as deep as five miles underground.

The first energy use of crude oil, which seeped out of the ground, was probably a burning torch. Looking for a cheaper source of light (as whale oil became too expensive), Edwin L. Drake drilled the first oil well in Pennsylvania in 1859. From that start, the oil industry has become the biggest industry in the world.

Petroleum is a mixture of chemicals in a family called hydrocarbons—compounds containing only hydrogen and carbon. A few of the lighter ones are easy to describe.

A methane molecule (CH_4) is made of one carbon atom surrounded by four hydrogen atoms. An ethane molecule (C_2H_6) is two attached carbons, propane (C_3H_8) is three, butane (C_4H_{10}) is four, and so on.

From this point, the compounds begin to get more complicated, with long and branching molecular chains that may have dozens of carbons, and even molecules in the shape of rings.

The liquid hydrocarbons in gasoline are usually five to ten carbon molecules, including octane (C_8H_{18}), which was once considered the best burning fuel. Today, octane rating in gasoline refers to different chemicals, including lead, which can be added to make gasoline burn better. Kerosene, used in lamps and to fuel jet engines, has molecule chains from ten to sixteen carbons long, and diesel fuel has chains that are longer still.

Every oil field has a slightly different crude oil, from thick and tarry to thin and greenish-brown. Some petroleum is almost pure hydrocarbons. Other batches are contaminated with sulfur.

Petroleum always appears in clean, sandy rock which once was underwater. Oil is found in Middle Eastern deserts, Texas, Alaska, the bottom of the North Sea and many other places. Most buried petroleum is under pressure, like the bubbles in a sealed bottle of soda. When it gets a chance, via cracks or wells drilled into the rock overhead, oil rises to the surface. Sometimes it even gushes into the air.

Crude petroleum wells may be more than a mile deep. If the pressure is great enough, oil rises to the surface by itself. If not, it is pumped, or water may be forced in to help the lighter oil rise.

All crude oil needs refining, which means cleaning and sorting the chemicals. First, technicians remove salt, sand, and water. As pressurized water fizzes through, it picks up the salt. Sand sinks, and the oil floats to the top.

Next, the crude is distilled in a fractionating tower. Because crude oil is a mixture of solids, liquids, and gases, it easily comes apart with heat. The lightest hydrocarbons float to the top of the tower.

Each fraction is trapped at a different level. From the top down, crude oil separates into methane and other gases, gasoline, kerosene, light oil, heavy oil, lubricators and waxes (such as petroleum jelly and paraffin), and the black asphalt used to pave streets.

The heavier products may be "cracked," or broken down chemically, into lighter molecules. A barrel of crude oil is only about 18 percent gasoline. Since Americans burn more than 100 billion gallons of gasoline each year, cracking helps increase the supply.

Heavier petroleum products can also be sold as motor oil, heating oil, or raw materials for the chemical industry. Thousands of different products are made from petroleum, from lipstick to fly spray.

Sometimes refineries are built close to oil fields. Other crude oil is loaded into trucks, train cars, or tanker ships. Underground pipelines carry about 10 percent. The Alaska pipeline, stretching for 800 miles across Alaskan wilderness (most of it above ground, to protect the frozen soil), carries 1.6 million barrels of oil per day. This is about 15 percent of the total United States production.

The United States is the second largest oil-producing nation (the Soviet Union is first), but we also import a large amount of oil from other countries. Part of the reason is to save our own supply for the future. At the rate the world is using oil, the easy-to-access sources will all be dry by early in the next century.

Tar deposits near the surface and oil trapped in spongelike shale rock still hold more than three trillion barrels of oil in the United States, alone. More complicated and more expensive drilling and mining methods will be needed to develop these sources.

Oil is less polluting than coal, but soot from unburned hydrocarbons causes dangerous and ugly air pollution. Another serious pollution problem is carbon dioxide. All fossil fuels add to the greenhouse effect.

Because oil floats on water, an oil spill is a major disaster. When an oil tanker ship crashes, or simply starts to leak, oil spreads out in a thin film, covering the top of the water for miles and miles around. Black, scummy deposits wash up on the beaches. Fish, animals, and

This sea otter almost died from pollution when oil from the 1989 Alaskan oil spill coated his fur. He was rescued and cleaned.

birds die by the thousands. Such a disaster happened in March 1989 when a tanker went aground near Alaska, spilling more than eleven million gallons of oil, polluting more than five thousand square miles of ocean, and killing a tremendous amount of wildlife.

Oil contains more potential energy per barrel than any other fossil fuel. Because it is liquid, oil is easy to ship and store. It is the best source of gasoline and the fuels needed to run automobiles, airplanes, and most kinds of engines. Its controlled burning inside combustion engines turns chemical energy into thermal energy and then into mechanical energy. Oil heats homes and buildings with thermal energy furnaces. Oil can also produce electrical energy. Oil's problems are expense, pollution, and the problem of limited supply.

Natural Gas

Natural gas comes from the same sources other fossil fuels do. A part of most oil wells and coal mines, natural gas can also be found alone. 25 percent of the United States energy supply comes from natural gas.

An invisible "air that burns" was discovered seeping out of the ground as long as 8,000 years ago in Iran. The Chinese first piped gas through bamboo tubes.

Natural gas deposits are harder to find than oil and coal. Wells may be five miles deep. Only about nine in a hundred wells drilled produce gas.

Mostly methane, natural gas contains a mixture of other light hydrocarbons—ethane, propane, and butane—plus some other gases from ancient volcanoes. Natural gas, itself, is colorless, odorless, and poisonous.

Natural gas is processed to remove water and valuable impurities like argon and helium gases. Propane and butane fuel lanterns, camp stoves, and even some heating burners. Processing removes all but the methane and ethane, and adds a small trace of a rotten-egglike odor so customers can tell when natural gas is leaking.

Most gas is transported by a million-mile network of pipelines. It may also be cooled until it turns to liquid natural gas (LNG), which takes up 600 times less space. LNG travels in refrigerated tank cars on ships, trains, or trucks. The United States is the second largest natural gas producer in the world (the Soviet Union is first), and we provide almost 95 percent of our own supply. Texas and Louisiana supply the most. Natural gas, like the other fossil fuels, is in limited supply.

Natural gas burns almost completely, without smoke or soot. Carbon dioxide is the only serious pollutant. Gas's main use is in homes, for heating and cooking, turning chemical energy into thermal, but it can also become electrical. More than half the homes in the country use gas heat.

Hydro Power

Falling water produces about 2 percent of the world's electric power, and about 10 percent in the United States. Water, as it falls, has enormous mechanical energy.

People first used water to move things from one place to another, but modern technology makes electricity a better use. Two conditions make hydro power possible: moving water, and a place for it to fall. Here are the typical steps:

1. Giant dams trap river water, which becomes a lake.
2. Gates open in the dam to let some water fall downstream.
3. Falling water turns the wheels of a turbine.
4. The turbine operates a dynamo.
5. Mechanical energy becomes electrical energy.

There are some problems connected with water energy. Hydro power does not cause pollution, but sometimes the dam causes flooding. Runs of fish often die because they cannot swim up-river to lay eggs. Sometimes disease-carrying mosquitoes thrive in the trapped water. Dams may also spoil a river's beauty.

Dam-building is expensive, but the power they provide justifies the investment. The use of hydro power is growing in some parts of the world. In the United States, the best rivers are already being used, but bigger dams could provide more electricity.

Nuclear Power

Nuclear power plants provide about 20 percent of the electricity used in the United States, 6 percent of our total power. About 400 plants are in operation around the world.

Nuclear power has a short history. It was invented in the United States in 1941 by Enrico Fermi and a group of physicists who made use of some amazing new discoveries about atoms and radioactivity.

The scientists knew that some atoms of the element uranium could be split in two, by shooting them with slow-moving neutrons. As they split, they gave off energy and something else: more neutrons.

Uranium-235 (U^{235}) is a radioactive atom with 92 protons and 143 neutrons (92 + 143 = 235). A radioactive atom sometimes gives off particles or bursts of energy, all by itself. In any lump of radioactive material, some atoms are always giving off energy. But shooting a slow neutron into an atom of U^{235} speeds up the process. The uranium fissions into two smaller atoms. Extra neutrons go flying off, carrying energy.

Fermi and his group invented a way to bring together enough U^{235}, called a critical mass, so that the neutrons flying out of one atom would split two or three more atoms. The neutrons flying out of those atoms would then split six to nine more atoms, and so on, until billions of atoms were splitting at the same time. They called it a chain reaction.

A nuclear bomb is a chain reaction gone wild. It explodes in a blinding flash of energy.

Nuclear power is a controlled chain reaction. It releases energy as heat, used to turn water into steam. From that point, the steps to making electricity are the same as for fossil fuels. Nuclear changes to thermal, then to mechanical, and finally to electrical energy. Safe use of a chain reaction is what nuclear power is all about.

A nuclear power plant needs fuel. Uranium, the usual choice, is a radioactive metal found in rock, soil, and seawater, in many parts of the world. Most of the easy-to-mine deposits in the United States are already used up, but huge amounts of low grade ore—less than one percent uranium—are being mined in several western states.

Uranium goes through colorful steps, from the ground to the power plant. First a black ore is dug out of deep mines or shallow pits. Technicians grind it and chemically extract a compound called "yellowcake." Yellowcake, poisonous but not very radioactive, is shipped in drums to enrichment plants. It is refined to pure "orange oxide," treated with fluoride to produce "green salt," and converted into a colorless crystal.

About 99 percent of all uranium atoms are uranium-238 (U^{238}) atoms (92 protons and 146 neutrons), which do not fission. U^{235} atoms, which do, make up one percent. Using some complex procedures, the enrichment plant extracts U^{235} atoms from one batch and adds them to another, until the U^{235} level measures about 3 percent. This enriched uranium is pressed into perfectly shaped pellets, loaded into metal tubes, and assembled into fuel rods. Each pellet, the size of a large vitamin pill, contains as much energy as a ton of coal.

New fuel rods are not dangerously radioactive. They can be safely handled and shipped. A nuclear power plant needs only a few truckloads of fuel a year.

Inside the power plant is the nuclear reactor. Fuel rods are loaded into the core of the reactor, surrounded by control rods, water, and thick steel and concrete walls. The movable control rods regulate the chain reaction by absorbing neutrons. Operators slide them out to speed up the reaction and back in to slow it down. An extra set of control rods, for emergencies, can close down the reaction completely.

The water slows down flying neutrons (slow neutrons fission best), cools the reactor, and transfers heat to the steam generator. The same water, more than 300,000 gallons per minute, is recycled again and again. It becomes highly radioactive.

Water in the steam generator runs the dynamo. This water is under pressure, so it can hold more heat. It is also recycled.

A third batch of water, usually taken from a nearby river and used just for cooling, never touches the reactor core. It is returned to the river, making the river warmer but not radioactive.

Losing its coolant water is the worst emergency a nuclear reactor faces. The core produces temperatures so high the metals would melt without constant cooling, even when the reactor is shut down. The accident at Three Mile Island, Pennsylvania, in 1979, was a loss-of-coolant emergency.

As the fuel rods produce heat, they become more—not less—radioactive. The chain reaction produces some highly radioactive waste products which begin to "poison" the uranium supply. Fuel rods must be removed and replaced after about three years. Workers handle

A generating plant uses nuclear energy to produce electricity.

them carefully, because spent nuclear fuel rods are among the most dangerously radioactive objects in the world.

The rods are lowered into a large pool of water, to sit until the worst radiation decays away. This takes about twenty years. After that, the rods, still dangerous, need to be stored somewhere. So far, all the waste from all the nuclear plants in the country is still sitting in pools.

At first, nuclear engineers thought the used fuel rods would be recycled to save the large amounts of unused uranium inside. Unfortunately, that turned out to be much more difficult than they thought. Today, what to do with nuclear waste is a serious problem. The government now plans to build a repository to hold the waste at Yucca Mountain, Nevada.

Nuclear energy is used to make electricity and to power some large ships. A well-run plant gives off neither air pollution nor carbon dioxide.

But nuclear power makes some people worry. There are four main reasons for this concern. One, a nuclear accident such as the one in 1986 at Chernobyl in the Soviet Union, could cause cancer and contamination over a wide area of land. Two, some nuclear plants may not be as safely run as they should be. Three, nuclear plants, because of safety rules and other reasons, have grown almost too expensive to build. And finally, nuclear waste is a serious problem that has not yet been solved.

Other Sources of Energy

Solar, wind, and tidal power, geothermal and biomass energy, and others, so far, do not provide enough energy to count in the big energy picture. Together, they provide less than one percent of the energy Americans use.

Money—not technology—is the biggest problem. Until the price of fossil fuel goes up (which it will as the supply runs out), new-but-more-expensive sources will not play an important role. In the future, our energy choices will become more and more important.

4

Energy and the People Who Use It

Think about camping—not in a gasoline-burning trailer, but in a small canvas shelter. Imagine you do not have batteries, propane stoves, or plastic coolers. How will you cook and store food? How will you keep warm—or cool, or clean, or dry? How will you see in the dark? What do you do for recreation?

Millions of people live that way. In places like Afghanistan and Ethiopia, for instance, many families use almost no energy but their own. Even in our country, either from poverty or choice, some people have very low-energy lifestyles.

Most Americans, on the other hand, use huge amounts of energy to live the way we like to live. The United States, with about 6 percent of the world's population, uses more than 30 percent of the world's energy. We consume more than any other country—more than all of Europe, more than all of Africa, more than most of the rest of the world put together.

We also produce more energy than any other country except the U.S.S.R. About 23 percent of the world's energy is developed in the

United States. Since Americans use even more than they produce, a large amount of energy has to be imported from other countries.

Measuring Energy

Saying that the United States produces and uses more energy than other countries can be confusing. How much more? How does a barrel of oil compare to a ton of coal or other kinds of energy?

Scientists use special units to describe energy. A British Thermal Unit, BTU, is a small quantity of heat from any source. One BTU equals 252 gram calories, or about as much heat as you get from one wooden kitchen match. One thousand BTU's is about the same amount of energy you use in one hour of bicycling or gain in eating one candy bar.

Americans produced nearly 66,000,000,000,000,000 (sixty-six quadrillion) BTU's in 1988. Quadrillions of BTU's can be abbreviated to quads.

One quadrillion is a thousand trillion, and one quad of energy is equal to 44 million tons of coal, 170 million barrels of oil, or eight billion gallons of gasoline. Americans used almost 80 quads of energy of 1988.

Most of those quads, about 40 percent, run factories and other kinds of industry. Another 25 percent go for all kinds of transportation, from the family station wagon to ships and trains. That leaves 35 percent to spend on heat and lights and air conditioning and all the other energy needs people have.

Electricity uses another set of units. A watt (W) is a very small unit of power. Just lighting the bulb in the oven takes 40 watts, so scientists normally talk about thousands of watts, or kilowatts (kW). Electric companies bill their customers on kilowatt-hours—the number of kilowatts used per hour, multiplied by the number of hours. One kW-hr equals 3,413 BTUs.

A hair dryer uses up about 25 kW-hrs in a year. A color television may use 300 to 400, and a freezer takes over 1000 kW-hrs per year to run. An average American household uses about 1,500 kW a month. When engineers plan a city's needs, kilowatts are not big enough. They talk in megawatts (MW or 1000 kW), and gigawatts, (GW, 1000 MW, or one billion watts). One gigawatt provides enough power for half a million people.

American cities consume a large fraction of the world's energy supply. But modern cities could not exist without reliable sources of power.

Energy Costs: Monetary

Energy costs money, but the cost is always changing. Gasoline stations usually have their prices per gallon printed on large signs and on each pump. The cost of gasoline goes up or down according to the world-wide price of a barrel of oil.

A group of Middle Eastern, African, and South American countries called the Organization of Petroleum Exporting Countries, or OPEC, sets the world price and supply. In 1973, OPEC started a major energy crisis by raising oil prices and cutting back production. Gasoline became so scarce, people lined up around the block for a chance to fill their tank, and hundreds of stations closed down.

Prices doubled and then doubled again. In just a few years, the cost of a barrel of oil went from $3.00 to $30.00.

One thing brought prices back down. People began to use less oil and gasoline. OPEC found itself with oil no one wanted, and prices dropped—not all the way back, but lower. In early 1990, oil was selling for $18 per barrel, but threats of war, in August, caused a rise.

Electric power prices are just as complicated. Each town or area has one local electric company, whose prices are controlled by law. They may produce the electricity they sell, or they may buy some or all of it from a huge network of wires and power plants, called a grid, strung all across the country and into Canada.

In March, 1989, electricity in Chicago homes cost 9.21 cents per kilowatt-hour. In Pittsburgh, electricity was selling for 10.5 cents; in New Orleans, 7.1; and in Seattle, 3.24 cents per kilowatt-hour. This means a color television set which may cost $10 to $20 a year to operate in Seattle, can cost more than $50 if you live in Pittsburgh.

The differences come from how the electricity is produced. Seattle uses almost 95 percent hydroelectric power—the cheapest. Chicago's electricity is 76 percent nuclear, 22 percent coal and not quite 2 percent oil and gas. In Pittsburgh, 70 percent coal and 30 percent nuclear results in a slightly higher price. New Orleans buys power from a mixture of sources. Prices change often, especially with the season. In summer, for instance, Chicago's rate goes up to 12.26 cents. The cost of nuclear power varies from plant to plant. Some well run nuclear plants make inexpensive electricity. Some other plants, tangled up in safety and political problems, cost far more to run. And some nuclear plants have cost so much to build, they are too expensive to run at all.

In 1988, one of the hottest, driest summers in history, people across the country used far more power than their electric companies had expected. At the same time, low rivers generated less hydro power and didn't have enough water to float barges filled with the coal and

Complex electronic equipment inside an electric transfer substation directs electricity from the place it is generated to places it is needed.

oil needed to generate emergency power. The electric companies had to buy extra power wherever they could find it—sometimes at costs much higher than usual. Prices went up.

Electricity must be generated as it is used, moving at the speed of light over high-energy transmission lines, heading in all directions. It cannot be stored, so if the supply at any time falls short, blackouts and brownouts happen. A blackout, when the electricity goes off completely, usually means an equipment problem, such as results from storm damage. A brownout, when lights flicker and dim, means not enough electricity is available.

Energy Spending

The United States spends about 11.2 percent of its gross national product—its total income as a country—on energy. In 1988, we spent more than $38 billion just for imported oil.

The amount of money Americans spend on energy is a problem for two reasons. One, energy costs hurt the United States in trading with other countries. Japan, for example, spends only 5 percent of its gross national product on energy—less than half the percentage we spend. That difference helps Japanese companies build cars, televisions, and computer parts cheaper than American companies can.

Two, energy costs hurt people. Money spent on a high electric, gasoline, or natural gas heating bill could be used, instead, on other things the family wants or needs. The national economy is affected.

Low-income Americans are hurt the most. Like food, energy is a need. People have to have it, whether they can afford it or not. A family with an income of only $5,000 a year spends a far higher percentage of its money on energy than a family with a $50,000 salary. In some states the average electric bill is over $60 a month.

Energy Costs: Political

It is not just by coincidence that the United States and the Soviet Union, the two most powerful countries in the world, also produce the most energy. Energy is power.

History is full of examples of energy mixed with politics. Wars are usually won by the side with the most energy resources, and long wars always are. Coal and other fuel to keep the trains moving helped the North win the American Civil War. A lack of gasoline in strategic locations led to Hitler's defeat in World War II.

Petroleum is a controlling factor in today's international politics, proven by Iraq's 1990 invasion of Kuwait. Small Middle-Eastern countries such as Saudi Arabia, Iran, and Lebanon have become world powers simply because they control a large percentage of the world's oil supply. Oil-producing countries sometimes use petroleum as a weapon, refusing to sell oil to other countries who disagree with them politically. Huge jumps in the price of oil can also be a weapon, forcing countries to pay too much or risk running short of energy. This is economic blackmail.

The United States, which uses more energy than any other country, has been caught in the past in political price wars. The more energy we use, the more vulnerable we are to energy politics and the more dangerous a weapon energy can be.

Energy Costs: Environmental

Using too much energy costs more than just money. It hurts the environment. It hurts the whole world. As we noted in Chapter 2, each source of energy causes some kind of pollution. Burning coal, oil, and gasoline puts tons of harmful chemicals into the atmosphere. These pollutants hang in the air as smog, kill trees, turn lakes as acidic as lemonade, and make people sick. Mining and drilling release pollution, too.

All fossil fuels give off carbon dioxide. Every year, 5.4 billion tons of CO_2, from the burning of coal, oil, natural gas, and wood, goes into the atmosphere—more than a ton for each person on the planet. By the year 2030, the blanket of air around earth will probably have twice as much carbon dioxide as it did two hundred years ago. That blanket will trap heat, warming and drying the whole world.

Some scientists think the greenhouse effect is already beginning to change weather on earth. They think it helped make summer 1988 so hot and dry. Other scientists are not so sure. But everyone agrees that clogging the atmosphere with more and more CO_2 is taking a big risk.

Nuclear energy does not give off carbon dioxide or smog into the air, but it produces dangerously radioactive waste products which will have to be stored for millions of years. The wastes from mining and refining uranium also leave radiation behind. Finally, nuclear energy causes people to worry, because a serious accident in a reactor's core could possibly pollute a state-sized area with radiation (as it did in the Soviet Union in 1986) and release deadly amounts of radiation into the air.

Hydro power does not give off air pollution, but dam-building makes important changes in the environment. Every kind of energy causes some kind of problem. No energy is free.

What Is Conservation?

One answer to these problems—national costs, personal costs, and environmental costs—is using less energy, or energy conservation. The less energy people use, the less the cost.

In 1973, during the worst energy crisis the United States ever faced, energy conservation was a top priority. Every unnecessary use of energy was considered wasteful, even electric Christmas decorations. Many cities stopped lighting streetlights. People began to buy smaller cars that burned less gasoline.

The government made new rules about what days people could buy gasoline and how warm buildings could be. People even talked about rationing gasoline, which means selling a specified amount to each customer, even if they need more.

The effort worked. Gasoline use dropped more than 11 percent. Use of electricity slowed. Since 1973, the world has saved far more energy than it has gained from all the new sources put together.

But some practices went too far. Dark streets led to falls and accidents. Some small cars turned out to be dangerous. In many places, people conserved so much power that the gas and electric companies had to raise prices because they were selling so little. Paying more, while using less, made everyone unhappy. Conservation began to seem like an unpleasant chore, or a punishment.

Why People Conserve Energy

For more than ten years, the overall amount of energy Americans used stayed about the same, even though the country added 20 million more homes and 50 million more cars and trucks. Then, in 1986, OPEC dropped the price of oil again. People stopped bothering so much about conservation. Factories started using more power. Cars grew bigger and faster—again.

The ups and downs of conservation are easy to follow. When energy prices go up, people conserve. When prices go down, people don't. And when new conservation ideas cost money, instead of saving it, people ignore them. Money seems to be the governing factor.

Some countries force conservation by putting a high tax on energy, especially gasoline, to keep people from using so much. That is not very popular in the United States. Our National Energy Policy Plan allows Americans to make their own "free and fully informed choices," about how much energy to use.

Choosing Conservation

Modern energy experts think the best plan is to look at conservation in a new way—not as a chore or punishment, but as a better way to do things. Being "energy efficient" doesn't mean being energy poor, but being energy smart. Energy efficiency means getting the most possible work from the least possible energy. Here are a few ideas, some new and some already at work:

1.   Building and buying more efficient cars, not just smaller ones.
       If every car got one-tenth of a mile more per gallon, millions

of gallons of gas would be saved. Ceramic (non-metal) engine parts and new engines designs are being tested. Some experts think every car could someday get 50 miles per gallon.

2. Building and buying energy-efficient houses. An average American family spends more than half its total energy dollar on home heating and water heating—for showers, laundry, and dishwashing. Homes built with well-insulated, tightly sealed doors and windows and well-designed heaters can save almost half that total. (Warning: well-insulated homes should be tested for radon gas.) Energy-efficient refrigerators and other appliances already in stores and homes can save even more. Unfortunately, they cost more to buy. The initial investment results in savings later.

3. Making older homes more energy efficient. This means sealing air leaks; putting in double windows; shading the sun in summer; using white paint in hot climates; changing to energy-saving fluorescent lights; and buying new, energy-efficient appliances. If every home made these changes, experts say, we could save more than five quads of energy every year.

4. Riding in a car pool or taking the bus. One car pool can save 20,000 gallons of gas a year.

5. Getting rid of energy waste. Waste and inefficiency, experts say, still steal almost half our total energy supply.

6. Helping big buildings and factories make energy-saving changes, including recycling and less packaging.

7. Planting trees around homes and buildings. Trees provide shade and cooling and use up carbon dioxide.

8. Turning the heat and the air conditioner down. Experts estimate that if everyone set his or her air conditioner thermostat up six degrees, 190,000 barrels of oil a day would be saved. Turning the heat down the same amount would save 570,000 barrels a day.

9. Turning down the heat and cooling even more at night and when you leave the house. (Some people think bringing the temperature back up or down later costs even more. Energy experts say they are wrong.)

10. Shaping up personal habits. Staring for long, undecided seconds into the wide open refrigerator and relaxing under leisurely, hot showers are not efficient uses of energy.

Conservation takes thought and practice. Basically, it means being careful to use only the needed amount of energy and no more.

Energy efficiency includes making sure all energy-using equipment is in good working order. It means recycling metal, glass, and paper, instead of expecting factories to make new. It means using less plastic to wrap everything. It means getting more for your money.

What Can You Do?

Do you know how much money your family spent on electricity last month? On heating? On gasoline? Find out. Can you think of a better use for some of that money? How can you make the bills smaller next month?

Do you know where your electric meter is located? Ask. Are the dials spinning? See if you can slow them down by turning things off. What would happen to the dials if you turned on all the televisions, stereos, and ovens at the same time? Your electric company probably has an information sheet to tell you how to read the meter to see how much electricity your household is using.

Find out what electricity costs per kilowatt-hour in your area. You can tell by reading the small print on your electric bill or by calling the power company. How much does it cost to burn a 100 watt lightbulb for ten hours at your house?

Hint: 100 watts multiplied by 10 hours = 1000 W-hr. Divide that by 1000 watts per kilowatt, 1000 divided by 1000 = 1 kW-hr. 1kW-hr, at your local cost per kW-hr, gives the answer.

Burning a 100 watt lightbulb ten hours in Seattle costs 3.24 cents and in Chicago, 9.2 cents. It doesn't seem like much, but think about

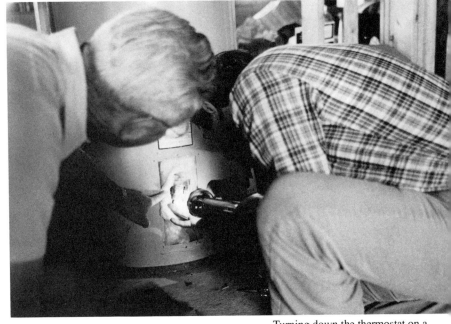

Turning down the thermostat on a hot water heater saves energy.

Energy-efficient appliances can conserve power. Not holding the door open too long can save even more.

all the lights, all over the house, all month long. Add in the stereo, the oven, the radio, and the television. Can you save money—and energy—by turning something off? You can save trees and lakes and fresh air, as well. You can help protect the United States from dependence on other countries for energy. Isn't it worth the trouble?

Some students at a California elementary school thought so. Just by turning off unused lights, they saved the school $1,000 per month. A school in Minnesota went further. They turned down the thermostats, closed the drapes to conserve heat, and got all the students and staff to help. They saved $16,000 the first year. Another California school district, which got a total energy audit of ideas from their local power company to help get rid of heat loss and waste, saved almost a million dollars.

Future Energy Needs
In spite of conservation, energy needs are always going up. From 1950 to 1973, world energy use more than tripled. Then growth slowed, but it didn't stop. By 1987, world energy production climbed to 321 quads, and energy planners are worried about the future.

The United States Department of Energy predicts that every part of the country will need at least 2 percent more power per year. In ten years, that means as much new power as 100 large power plants can generate. But new plants burning coal or using nuclear energy are not popular. No one wants one in his or her neighborhood, and even if that were not a problem the plants can take ten years or more to build.

Where will the power come from? Experts have several ideas, but one possibility is new sources of energy.

Other Sources of Energy
Right now, all other sources of energy combined, supply less than one quad. Sometimes you see numbers that look bigger, but those statistics always include hydro power, which is already counted in the big five.

But just because they cannot yet take over the power supply for a whole city does not mean that solar, geothermal, or other renewable sources of energy won't work for you and your family. In fact, they are working already, all over the country. The big five sources of energy may provide 99 percent of people's needs today, but that last one percent—from renewable energy—is especially important. It has the most room to grow.

Schoolchildren learning ways to conserve energy.

5

Energy Choices for the Future

Picture a home fifty years in the future. The roof, walls, and windows might all be made of special materials to trap sunlight for heating rooms and water. On especially cold or hot days, the furnace/air conditioner would burn gas made from household wastes.

Your car would run on a fuel made mostly of alcohol from plants, and electricity might be generated directly by the sun or the wind, the ocean tides, nuclear fusion, or the heat from a volcano—carried on superconducting wires that don't waste a single watt.

Some of these future possibilities are current actualities in the United States and other countries. They are called future choices only because they are not yet providing energy in large amounts—the technology to make them happen already exists. There are other choices still in the planning stages. To keep the world supplied with energy, we need all the solutions we can get.

Biomass

As people worry about running out of coal and oil, scientists are looking at an old source of energy in a new way. Biomass is a general term for living matter. Every year, enough of the sun's energy is stored by plants to supply ten times the amount of energy the world uses. This energy is renewable, because new plants are always growing.

Some people have always burned wood for fuel, but technology has some better ideas for getting energy from plants and other organic matter. Here are a few:

1. Turn corn into alcohol and add it to gasoline.
2. Turn animal manure and sewage into methane gas.
3. Press garbage into fuel pellets.
4. Burn leftover wood from logging and lumber-making.
5. Burn brush, leaves, and all kinds of plant "trash."

The first two provide chemical energy. The last three turn chemical energy into thermal energy. All try to use unwanted biomass, not food plants or the trees in the park.

Some experts say the United States could collect and use enough biomass to provide one-fourth of the country's total energy supply. It sounds easier than it is. Burning biomass products causes the same pollution problems as fossil fuels, and controlling pollution is expensive.

The biggest problem is that biomass material is not energy-efficient. To provide the same energy as a barrel of oil takes half a ton of wood or garbage. Supplying one city with all its electricity would take huge forests—or all the garbage in the country.

Used in smaller ways, biomass energy is already at work. In 1989, the first public gasohol—alcohol mixed with gas—station opened in Los Angeles. Several cities across the country are already producing heat and enough electricity for thousands of homes, using their own garbage as fuel.

Solar Energy

The sun is the world's main source of energy. It beams enough free light and heat to earth every day to supply all the world's energy needs. Unfortunately, except for sunbathing on the beach, using sunlight isn't free. Solar energy is radiant energy. Turning it into useful amounts of thermal and electrical energy requires complicated and expensive technology.

Right now, the most successful use of solar energy is for home water heating. Large, flat panels, installed on the roof of a house, hold water pipes which can supply that house with fifty to ninety percent of its hot water needs, even in not-very-sunny places. These solar collectors are available now, and the several thousand dollars they add to the price of a new house is returned quickly in the form of savings.

Home heating is available, too. A homeowner installs glass panels on the roof to collect and use sunlight. They work well, at least in sunnier parts of the country, but they are expensive to install. Most homes also need to have a fuel-burning furnace for times when the solar panels cannot provide enough heat.

Rooftop solar panels heat water for home use.

In 1988, a solar-powered car broke the world speed record for solar-powered cars of 48.7 mph. In 1989, another solar car drove all the way across the country. Someday, everyone may own one. Making electrical energy from sunlight is even more complicated. One idea uses huge fields covered with mirrors, which reflect energy to a steam generator inside a tower. The idea works, as long as the sun shines, but it costs more than ten times as much as using coal.

Photovoltaic cells can change sunlight directly into electricity, by using solar cells like the tiny batteries in watches and calculators. Light knocks loose electrons, to cause a small electric charge in two different materials inside the cell, and a tiny metal grid captures the electric current.

One photovoltaic plant is already operating near Sacramento, California, and another is generating electricity in Austin, Texas. Photovoltaic panels provide electricity to more than 15,000 homes in the United States, mostly vacation homes and remote ranches and cabins. Photovoltaic cells provide power to hospitals located far from other power sources, and they run remote phones and refrigerators, pumps and train signals.

Right now, photovoltaic electricity costs three times as much as other sources. Someday, scientists picture a giant space station, ten miles across, hovering over cities to produce solar electricity and beam it back to earth.

Wind Power
Wind power is another old idea. For hundreds of years people have been building windmills to capture the free energy blowing by. Modern windmills use winds of thirteen to fifteen miles per hour to turn turbines and change mechanical energy into electrical energy.

Wind turbines don't need fuel and they don't pollute the air, but they are noisy and sometimes interfere with television reception. They work only where the wind is stronger than average, and their biggest problem is the space they take up. Each giant windmill can supply only a few megawatts. Some energy planners hope someday to build 50,000 wind turbines in the midwestern plains, to supply more than 2 quads of energy. Hawaii, California, and some other locations are already giving them a try. Wind turbines work best in isolated spots where bringing in electricity by wire is too expensive.

Tide Power

Moving ocean tides supply another kind of water power. People have tried for hundreds of years to make use of the unlimited energy in tides, without much success. Now, projects in France, the Soviet Union, and Canada are using special turbines to turn the tide's mechanical energy into electrical energy. They don't pollute, but they only work at the ocean's shore, and they can cause flooding, destroy fish habitats, and spoil large beaches for other uses.

A wind turbine uses moving air currents to generate electricity.

Geothermal Energy

The inside of the earth is hot. Sometimes that heat, called geothermal energy, comes to the surface as hot springs, boiling geysers, or steaming volcanoes. Underground hot water can be used to heat houses. In Nevada and Idaho it is already in use, and in Iceland, geothermal energy is the main source of heat.

Hawaii is already using the heat inside volcanoes to generate electricity, a thermal to electrical energy change. Iceland, Japan, and Italy have been making geothermal electricity for years. Seven percent of California's electricity is geothermal.

Geothermal energy plants are super-efficient. They work at full speed, almost all the time. Unfortunately, the steam is not as hot as the steam from a fuel burning plant, so special turbines are needed. Nor is it as clean. Pollutants in the steam rust the machinery.

Geothermal energy gives off some bad-smelling sulfur pollution, but most of it can be trapped. The biggest problem: geothermal heat is only available in areas where the earth's inner heat has leaked close to the surface. Drilling opens a few more places, but most of the earth's heat is buried too deep to use. Experts estimate that 32 million quads of geothermal energy are within reach, waiting for people to find the best ways to use them.

Nuclear Fusion

Nuclear fusion, which powers the sun, is a popular future energy possibility. The idea is simple—fusing two atoms together—but the technology, so far, is so difficult that producing fusion uses up more energy than it gives off. Scientists in the United States, the Soviet Union, and other countries are working on the problems.

The fuel is special atoms of hydrogen called deuterium, which have one proton and one neutron in their nucleus (ordinary hydrogen has no neutron). Some techniques also use tritium, a kind of radioactive hydrogen with one proton and two neutrons. The idea is to heat them to temperatures hotter than the sun and hold them together for one second. But since temperatures that hot can melt any kind of container, scientists have to hold them with magnets. Research is still underway. Once scientists make it work, nuclear fusion should be an inexpensive, clean source of energy. The fuel, deuterium, will come from ocean water. The process will cause very little pollution. But right now, fusion is not in use anywhere.

New Plans for Coal

Research into coal technology offers some new ideas. In Georgia, powdered peanut hulls are being mixed with coal, to provide cheaper, cleaner electricity. In the Rocky Mountains, in early 1988, scientists tested a new method of carefully burying veins of coal in the ground to turn the coal into a clean-burning gas. The gas was piped to the surface and used to turn a turbine. Chemists in 1988 also developed a new method of turning coal into gasoline. These synthetic (man-made) fuels, called synfuels, cost too much to produce now, but they are ready if the prices of other kinds of energy rise.

Petroleum and coal are so similar chemically that almost anything petroleum can do, coal can be made to do also. But the chemical transformation, so far, is always more expensive than oil from a well.

Fuel Cells

A different way to use fossil fuels to make electricity is with a fuel cell. Fuel cells work like giant batteries. As oxygen reacts chemically with a fuel, electrons begin to move. As electrons flow one way through the battery, ions move the other. (Ions are the positively charged atoms which have lost electrons.) On their way, electrons transfer kinetic energy to a wire. Fuel cells convert chemical energy directly into electrical energy.

To work, fuel cells need completely clean fuel, such as natural gas or specially processed oil or coal. Since the fuel does not burn, the cells do not pollute. They have been used aboard United States space shuttles and to run electric cars. So far, they produce very expensive power, more than twice as expensive as burning gasoline.

Cogeneration

As factories and businesses burn coal or other fuels, sometimes they produce more heat than they need. That waste heat can be turned into electricity. Extra electricity can then be sold to power companies, for resale to other customers.

One example is a huge dairy production plant in California. The dairy produces 800 million gallons of milk, 80 million pounds of cheese, and 48,800 kW of power every year, by turning waste milk products into alcohol to use as fuel. Cogeneration is a form of conservation. It makes the best use of available energy.

High Temperature Superconductors

As electricity moves through power lines, sometimes as much as half of it disappears. It becomes useless heat, or entropy.

In 1986, scientists made some major discoveries about a new kind of electrical conductor—a superconductor which could carry electricity with no waste. Superconductors need to be kept cold to work, but not nearly so cold as physicists had once thought. Superconductors do not produce electricity, but they might someday be able to save so much current, they could cut energy needs by almost half.

It takes time and money to develop new sources of energy and to make old ones work more efficiently. Science and technology can do only part of the job. The more people know and care about the energy they use, the safer and more dependable our energy supply will be.

Glossary

AC (Alternating current)—Electrons vibrate along a wire, passing energy from atom to atom.

acid rain—Rain polluted with chemicals that react with water and fall to earth as acids.

anthracite—A clean-burning hard, black Pennsylvania coal.

atom—The smallest particle into which an element can be divided and still keep its identity. Atoms have a central nucleus, surrounded by moving electrons.

biomass—Animal and plant material, which can be used as fuel.

bituminous—The most common coal. Black and banded, it is found across the central and eastern United States.

BTU (British Thermal Unit)—The amount of energy needed to heat one pound of water, one degree Fahrenheit.

carbon—an element, atomic number 6, found in coal, diamonds, and all plant and animal tissue. Atomic weight, 12.01.

chemical bond—The strong attractive force that holds atoms together in molecules.

cogeneration—Producing electricity from industrial waste heat.

combustion—Burning. Combustion usually involves oxygen combining with fuel to produce heat and light.

DC (Direct current)—Electrons flow along a wire, carrying energy.

deuterium—An isotope (another form) of hydrogen, having one proton and one neutron in its nucleus. (Ordinary hydrogen has no neutron.) Atomic number 1, atomic weight 2.

dynamo—A machine that converts mechanical energy into electrical energy.

electricity—A negatively charged subatomic particle, 1/1837 the size of a proton.

element—A substance made up of atoms with the same atomic number, or number of protons in their nucleus. Some common elements are hydrogen, carbon, and gold.

entropy—A measure of the energy which becomes unavailable for use as energy changes form.

fossil fuels—Plant and animal materials that have changed form due to heat and pressure over thousands of years. Examples are coal and oil.

fuel cell—A device which changes chemical energy directly into electrical energy.

geothermal power—Electricity formed from the heat energy inside the earth.

gigawatt (GW)—One thousand megawatts, one million kilowatts, or one billion watts.

greenhouse effect—In gardening, a greenhouse uses glass or plastic windows to trap heat from the sun. Some scientists fear the growing percentage of carbon dioxide in the atmosphere could serve as a greenhouse to trap excess heat and make the whole earth hotter.

hydrocarbon—A chemical compound composed of hydrogen and carbon. The simplest hydrocarbon is methane, CH_4, but the two elements can form chains containing sixty atoms or more. Most hydrocarbons are used as fuels.

kilowatt (kW)—One thousand watts.

kilowatt-hour—The amount of energy used by a one-kilowatt appliance in one hour of operation.

kinetic energy—Energy of motion.

lignite—A smoky-burning, soft, brown western coal.

magnetism—One of the elementary forces of nature. It involves certain metals, such as iron, or current-carrying materials, and it causes atoms and their electrons to move in predictable ways. The earth is a giant magnet.

megawatt (MW)—One thousand kilowatts, or one million watts.

molecule—The smallest possible amount of any compound. A molecule may contain atoms of the same element or more than one element, held together by chemical bonds.

natural gas—A mixture of hydrocarbon gases, mostly methane, found in underground rock reservoirs. Natural gas is a clean-burning fuel.

neutron—A subatomic particle with no electrical charge, found in the nucleus of most atoms.

nuclear fission—The splitting of an atom's nucleus, to release energy.

nuclear fusion—The joining together of two atomic nuclei into one, to release energy.

nucleus—The central part of an atom, where most of the mass is concentrated. It has a positive charge equal to the number of protons present, which also equals the atomic number.

packing fraction—A calculated quantity for an atom which reflects the energy holding the nucleus together.

petroleum—A mixture of thick, naturally occurring oily liquids which can be made into fuel.

photon—A massless subatomic particle which carries energy. A particle of light.

potential energy—Stored energy.

radioactivity—The giving off, or radiating, of energy by the nuclei of unstable atoms.

sub-bituminous—A soft, black coal of the western United States.

superconductor—A material which can conduct electricity without losing energy in the process.

synfuel—petroleum and natural gaslike materials manufactured artificially, usually from coal.

thermodynamics—The branch of physics involved with heat transfer and the changing of energy from one form to another.

turbine—A device for generating mechanical power from moving fluids, such as steam or water falling over a dam.

uranium—A poisonous metallic element, atomic number 92, which can produce energy due to radioactivity. Atomic weight, 238.03.

watt—A unit of power, defined as one joule per second, or a certain very small amount of work done in one second.

Further Reading

Asimov, Isaac. *The History of Physics*. New York: Walker & Company, 1984.

Golden, Augusta. *Small Energy Sources: Choices That Work*. San Diego: Harcourt Brace Jovanovich, 1988.

Haines, Gail Kay. *The Great Nuclear Power Debate*. New York: The Putnam Publishing Group, 1985.

Purcell, John. *From Hand Ax to Laser: Man's Growing Mastery of Energy*. New York: Vanguard, 1982.

Schobert, Harold. *Coal: The Energy Source of the Past and Future*. Washington, DC: American Chemical Society, 1987.

Smith, Norman F. *Energy Isn't Easy*. New York: Coward-McCann, 1984.

Woodburn, John H. *Opportunities in Energy Careers*. Lincolnwood, Ill.: VGM Career Horizons, 1985.

For Further Information

CAREIRS Conservation and Renewable Energy Inquiry and Referral Service. It answers questions for the general public by toll-free phone or mail.

Renewable Energy Information
P.O. Box 8900
Silver Spring, Maryland 20907
1-800-523-2929
1-800-462-4983
(in Pennsylvania)
1-800-233-3071
(in Alaska and Hawaii)

NATAS National Appropriate Technology Assistance Service. It has specialists available to give tailored answers to specific questions about appliance use, home construction, conservation, etc., by toll-free phone or mail.
NATAS
U.S. Department of Energy
P.O. Box 2525
Butte, Montana, 59702-2525
1-800-428-2525
1-800-428-1718

NEIC National Energy Information Center. It gives information on energy production, consumption, prices, and supplies, by phone or mail.

National Energy Information Center
U.S. Department of Energy
Forrestal Building, E1-22
Room 1F048
1000 Independence Avenue, SW
Washington, DC 20585
1-202-252-8800

Other agencies providing information:

Alliance To Save Energy
1925 K Street NW, Suite 206
Washington, DC 20006

Solar Energy Research Institute
1617 Cold Boulevard
Golden, CO 80401

Electric Power Research Institute
3412 Hillview Avenue
P.O. Box 10412
Palo Alto, CA 94303

Index

About the Author

Gail B. Haines is the author of a number of science books for young people. In 1989 she won a Science Writing Award from the American Institute of Physics and a Washington Governor's Award for Science Writing. Her writing career is inspired by her enjoyment of reading about science. An active Girl Scout, Mrs. Haines now serves on the National Board of Directors of the Girl Scouts of the U.S.A. She and her husband have two children and live in Olympia, Washington.